Al Capone
was a
GOLfeR

Al Capone was a GOLfeR

Hundreds of Fascinating Facts from the World of Golf

Erin Barrett and
Jack Mingo

CONARI PRESS
Berkeley, California

Conari Press books are distributed by Publishers Group West.

Cover Illustration: Colin Johnson
Cover and Book Design: Claudia Smelser
Author Photo: Jen Fariello

Library of Congress Cataloging-in-Publication Data

Barrett, Erin.
    Al Capone was a golfer : hundreds of fascinating facts from the
    world of golf / Erin Barrett and Jack Mingo.
        p.   cm. —(Totally riveting utterly entertaining trivia)
    Includes bibliographical references.
    ISBN 1-57324-720-0
    1. Golf—Miscellanea. I. Title: Hundreds of fascinating facts
    from the world of golf. II. Mingo, Jack. III. Title. IV. Series.
GV967 .B325 2002
796.352—dc21   2002000888

Printed in the United States of America.

02 03 DATA 10 9 8 7 6 5 4 3 2 1

Al Capone was a GOLfeR

A Word from the Authors

Clearly, it's easy to lose perspective about a game like golf. Golf combines so many variables, from weather and course design to individual players' physical abilities and mental attitude, that every round is different. Are fanatic golfers best envied or pitied? Have they found the secret of living large, or are they escaping from it? Are a driver, a putter, and a sunny day the keys to wisdom or the distractions that will forever keep someone from attaining it?

These are all questions that every golfer must grapple with. Thank heavens, however, we don't do that here. Instead, we offer arcane trivia, celebrity anecdotes, fun facts, and quotes from the best and worst golfers you've ever heard of. If you want to wrestle with the meaning behind the game of golf or learn how to psychically become one with your driver on a par 5, go buy another book. But if you want to know why they're called "duffers," who has driven a golf ball more than a mile, and what it took to make Groucho Marx throw his golf clubs over a cliff at Cypress Point . . . well, this is your book. (Or at least it will be, when you take it up to the register and actually pay for it.)

Enjoy!

Erin Barrett
Jack Mingo

one

Golf Is . . .

AFTER A BAD DAY'S GOLF.

"**G**olf is a puzzle without an answer."

—Gary Player

"**G**olf is an expensive way of playing marbles."

—G. K. Chesterton, author

"**G**olf is the Lord's punishment for man's sins."

—James Reston, journalist

"**G**olf is a game with the soul of a 1956 Rotarian."

—Bill Mandel, Berkeley radio legend

"**G**olf is a game of expletives not deleted."

—Dr. Irving J. Gladstone, golfer

"**G**olf is an ideal diversion, but a ruinous disease."

—Bertie Charles Forbes

"**G**olf is the hardest game in the world to play, and the easiest to cheat at."

—Dave Hill, pro golfer

"**G**olf is so popular simply because it is the best game in the world at which to be bad."

—A. A. Milne

"Golf is a game whose aim is to hit a very small ball into an even smaller hole, with weapons singularly ill-designed for the purpose."

—*Winston Churchill*

"**G**olf is like faith: It is the substance of things hoped for, the evidence of things not seen."

—Arnold Haultain,
Canadian author (1857–1941)

"**G**olf is the most fun you can have without taking your clothes off."

—Chi Chi Rodriguez

"**G**olf is a wonderful exercise. You can stand on your feet for hours, watching somebody else putt."

—Will Rogers

"**G**olf is essentially an exercise in masochism conducted out of doors."

—Paul O'Neil

"Golf is war. And like all wars, if you're not looking to win, you probably shouldn't show up."

> —*Capt. Bruce Waren Ollstein,*
> *author and golf strategist*

"Golf is a game where the ball always lies poorly and the player always lies well."

> —*Anonymous golfer*

"Golf is not just exercise: It is an adventure, a romance . . . a Shakespeare play in which disaster and comedy are intertwined and you have to live with the consequences."

> —*Harold Segall, golfer*

"Golf is a game that creates emotions that sometimes cannot be sustained with the club still in one hand."

—Bobby Jones

"Golf is 20 percent mechanics and technique. The other 80 percent is philosophy, humor, tragedy, romance, melodrama, companionship, camaraderie, cussedness, and conversation."

—Grantland Rice, American sportswriter

"Golf is the hardest game in the world. There is no way you can ever get it. Just when you think you do, the game jumps up and puts you in your place."

—Ben Crenshaw

"Golf is an awkward set of bodily contortions designed to produce a graceful result."

—*Thomas Armour, golfer*

"Golf is good for the soul. You get so mad at yourself you forget to hate your enemies."

—*Will Rogers*

"Golf is like a cat chasing its tail. You're never going to catch it. The day you think you've got your game down pat, something goes awry and you're back to square one. That's one reason why I love the game so much: the soul-searching, and the never-ending search for the perfect swing."

—*Greg Norman*

"Golf is an exercise which is much used by the Gentlemen in Scotland. A large common, in which there are several little holes, is chosen for the purpose. It is played with little leather balls stuffed with feathers, and sticks tipped with horn. . . . A man would live ten years the longer for using this exercise once or twice a week."

—*Dr. Benjamin Rush (1770)*

"Golf is not a game of great shots. It's a game of the most accurate misses."

—*Gene Littler*

"Golf is like a horse—If you take your eye off it, it'll jump back and kick your shins for you."

—*Byron Nelson*

"**G**olf is a game of endless predicaments."

—*Chi Chi Rodriguez*

"**G**olf is not a fair game. It's a rude game."

—*Fuzzy Zoeller*

"**G**olf is 20 percent talent and 80 percent management."

—*Ben Hogan*

"**G**olf is not so much a game as it is a creed and a religion."

—*Arnold Haultain*

"**G**olf is meant to be fun."

—*Jack Nicklaus*

"Golf is just a game, and an idiotic one at that."

—Mark Calcavecchia (after failing to make the cut at the British Open)

"Golf is a game where guts, stick-to-it-ness, and blind devotion will get you nothing but an ulcer."

—Tommy Bolt

two

Driving and Putting Through History

Who invented golf? We could go with the Scots, but it's not that easy. The simple fact is that hitting a rock into a hole in the ground is such a no-brainer concept for a game that dozens of nationalities can lay claim to having invented it. Evidence shows exactly that—that the basic game was invented over and over again all over the world.

The Visigoths—known for their plundering and overall pillaging—may have played golf before they overthrew ancient Rome on August 4, 410. But whether they knew of the game before the sack of Rome, this very unrefined lot, many historians believe, certainly played the golf-like game of *paganica* afterward.

According to historian Ling Hong-ling, the Chinese played a game very much like modern golf five centuries before the Scots. *Chuiwan* ("hitting ball") was depicted in tenth-century pottery designs and paintings and mentioned in a document that dates back to A.D. 943. Hong-ling believes that early travelers brought the game back to Europe. The game's popularity died out in the 1500s, a few decades after the game was "invented" in Scotland.

French people swear that golf came from their ancient game called *Jeu de Mail*.

Golf also might've come from an early British game called *knur and spell*.

Belgium's game called *chole* goes back to the 1300s. Although similar to golf, both sides played the same ball, and at certain intervals, the opposing team had the opportunity to hit the ball into any available hazard.

The Dutch game of *kolven,* which was played on any surface including ice, may have been golf's predecessor. The supporters of this theory insist that the word *tee* came from the old Dutch *tuitje* (pronounced "toytee"), meaning "mound;" *golf* came from *kolfe* ("club"); and *putt* came from *put* ("hole").

Kolven at least has the distinction of being the first golf-like game played by colonists in the New World: Historians have found a warrant from 1657 for the arrest of three Dutch immigrants in Fort Orange (now Albany, New York), charged with skipping church and playing kolven on Sunday.

Two years later, Fort Orange issued an ordinance to "forbid all persons from playing 'het kolven' in the streets."

Whatever its earlier roots, linguists say that the word *golf* comes from an ancient Scottish word *gowf* that meant "to strike."

What the L!: *Goiff* and *goff* were the preferred spelling and pronunciation of "golf" during the 1500s and the 1600s.

Regardless, golf eventually emerged in Scotland. Whether it was indigenous or—like kilts and the bagpipe—imported from somewhere else, the game became so popular that King James II feared that his army was spending too much time playing it instead of practicing their archery. On March 6, 1457, he decreed that "Fute-ball and Golfe be utterly cryed down" (banned) as a threat to his army's readiness to do battle against England.

King James IV reaffirmed the embargo in 1491. However, it was a "Do as I say, not as I do" situation—he is the first player of golf for whom we have documentation. A notation in the Lord High Treasurer's accounts shows payment of 14 shillings to a bowmaker for making "the King's golf clubbis and ballis." From that point on, the treasurer's records showed numerous golf-related expenses for replacement balls and even a gambling debt to the Earl of Bothwell for 14 shillings lost on the links.

After a peace treaty with England, Scotland's ban against golf was finally rescinded by King James IV in 1503, except "in tyme of sermonis" on Sunday.

Perhaps King James should've kept the ban. Scots became very good at golf . . . but their archery abilities got rusty. When the 1503 peace treaty fell apart ten years later, the Scots suffered bloody defeat by English archers at the Battle of Flodden in 1513. Scotland lost not only many men and a number of their royals but a king as well: King James IV was killed in battle.

Church records from Scotland in the six-teenth century show that parishioners were severely fined the first two times they were caught playing golf on the Sabbath. The third time, they were excommunicated.

King James IV's notorious granddaughter, Mary, Queen of Scots, was the first known female golfer. Before she lost her head for other reasons, she gave her life to golf. History tells it that when Mary Queen of Scots heard the news of the murder of her husband (who also happened to be her cousin), she was in the middle of a game of golf. By all accounts, she scandalized her subjects and the clergy by continuing to play her round, and then playing again just a few days later. (The fact that she hated her husband, likely arranged his murder, and then married his murderer just three months later didn't help, either.)

Mary's son, James VI, was also an avid golfer. He spread the habit to England when he became its king. As England's James I, he helped heal the church/golf split, in that he was the King James who authorized the first English translation of the Bible.

James I made two golf-related proclamations. One appointed William Moyer, an expert crafter of bows, as Royal Golf Club

Maker. The other forbid the purchase of golf balls from Holland, upon which golfers were spending "no small quantitie of golde and silver," and assigned a twenty-one-year monopoly of ball making to one James Melvil. (This latter proclamation some historians point to as evidence of golf's Dutch origins.)

Despite golf's popularity in the fourteenth and fifteenth centuries, it took some 150 years before the game became institutionalized and formalized. In 1744, the Company of Gentlemen Golfers of Leith (Scotland) became the first golf organization, and their thirteen rules were the earliest known written golf code.

The original thirteen written rules of golf had a few variations from the ones we play now. For one, the green of the previous hole was the tee of the next hole—players were to start within a club's length from the last hole. Once a ball was played on a hole, no substitute ball could be introduced. And if a player lifted his ball out of water or "watery filth," his opponent got to play an extra stroke.

What is now known as the Royal and Ancient Golf Club of St. Andrews wasn't formed until ten years later. In 1754, its twenty-two founding members adopted golf rules that were almost identical to the Leith Club's. St. Andrews' many holes proved more popular than Leith's five, which eventually led to the standardization of the golf game to conform to St. Andrews'.

Still, golfing organizations didn't exactly go "Fore!" and multiply. In 1864, more than a century later, there were only thirty-three known golfing clubs—thirty in Scotland and three in England.

The first permanent golfing club in the Western Hemisphere was the Royal Montreal Golf Club, which was established in 1873.

The first golf club in the United States? It's in dispute. The Oakhurst (West Virginia)

Golf Club is said, without documentation, to have had a founding date of 1884. The Dorset (Vermont) Field Club has equally undocumented claims that it was organized in 1886. Our call on the whole mess? The Foxburg (Pennsylvania) Golf Course, which has documentation to show that its golf course was built in 1885 and its charter became formalized in 1887.

It wasn't until the end of the nineteenth century that golf took off like a straight shot to the green. By 1900 there were golfing organizations all over the world and more than 2,000 in England alone.

The first professional golf tournament was sponsored by the Prestwick (Scotland)

Golf Course in 1860. Called the Open Championship, it attracted eight professional golfers and a considerable degree of skepticism: after all, could somebody playing for money be trusted to abide by the rules of the game, since a true gentleman played only for the honor of winning?

The Prestwick competition eventually became known as the British Open, the name it bears today.

Early golfing clubs were as dedicated to drinking as they were to driving . . . which helps explain why the British Open trophy is a claret jug.

The early days of the British Open consisted of playing the same nine holes four times in a single day. Ending before dark was always a challenge, so it became a tradition for frontrunners to bribe poorly scoring competitors to quit early and speed up the game.

The very first golf manual was published in England. Written by H. B. Farnie in 1857, it was called—sensibly enough—*The Golfer's Manual.*

The first American book on golf, *Golf in America: A Practical Manual,* was published in 1895. Up until that point, most Americans were terribly confused by the game, as inadvertently revealed by an explanatory article in the *Philadelphia Times:*

> It is sometimes agreed that the game shall be won by him who makes the largest number of holes within a given number of minutes, say twenty or thirty. . . . Each player places his ball at the edge of a hole designated as a starting point. He then bats it . . . toward the next hole. As soon as it has started he runs forward . . . and his servant, who is called "caddy," runs after him. . . .

As far as anyone knows, the first photo of someone playing golf in the United States was taken in 1888.

Horace L. Hotchkiss was in his sixties when he organized the first seniors' golf tournament at the Apawamis Club in Rye, New York, in 1905, attempting to prove that golf wasn't just a young person's game. It was a huge success, and the United States Seniors Golf Association was formed twelve years later.

The Ryder Cup was started in 1926 by Samuel Ryder, a wealthy English business-man who made his fortune from selling penny packets of flower seeds.

Samuel Ryder's idea of good prize money? "I'll give $5 to each of the winning players," he offered. "And I'll give a party afterwards, with champagne and chicken sandwiches." Eventually he was convinced to put up $250 for a solid gold trophy instead.

three

Golf by the Numbers

"**G**olf is a game in which you shout
'Fore,' shoot six and write down five."

—*Paul Harvey*

1 in 8,606: One often-repeated estimate as to the odds of making a hole-in-one—that averages out to one in every 478 rounds.

1 in 13,000: The estimate of companies that sell hole-in-one prize insurance to golf tournament organizers, or about one in every 722 rounds.

According to the Professional Golfers Association (PGA), a male professional's or a top amateur player's chances are 3,708 to 1 (an average of one hole-in-one every 206 rounds); a female pro's odds are 4,648 to 1 (one every 258 rounds). However, the average player's odds are only 42,952 to 1 (one every 2,386 rounds).

49: Holes-in-one made by golf pro Mancil Davis, who had more in his career than any other pro.

$85.70: The average cost of a weekend's green fees in Hawaii, the most expensive state in which to play golf.

$23.80: The average cost of a weekend's green fees in South Dakota, the cheapest state in which to play golf.

6: Tiger Woods' age when he got his first hole-in-one. However, at the time he failed to beat the record for youngest hole-in-one, which had been set by a five-year-old.

3: The age, in 2001, of Jake Paine of Lake Forest, California, who smashed Tiger Woods' record. He teed off with his Snoopy driver and hit the ball a soaring and rolling 48 yards, directly into the cup.

$180,000: The initiation fee of the most expensive golf and country club in the United States, not including monthly dues. The club in question is the Vintage Club of Indian Wells, California.

$900,000: The amount awarded to Retief Goosen for winning the U.S. Open in 2001.

$500: The amount awarded to Gene Sarazen for winning the U.S. Open in 1922.

$28,000: The price of a four-passenger, fully loaded deluxe Deusenberg Estate Golf Car, including CD players and rack-and-pinion steering.

101 mph: The speed that a driver travels when swung by a typical "accomplished" golfer.

7: The world record for the number of golf balls balanced on top of each other.

10 percent: The percentage of all professional golfers who are single and unattached.

35: The mean age of those players who tour with the PGA.

7 feet: The minimum height that the United States Golf Association (USGA) calls an adequate flag stick.

90: The compression number of a normal golf ball. The compression number measures the springiness of the ball. In windy or hot conditions, a ball should be harder, with a compression number of about 100.

12 percent: The percentage of all lightning fatalities that happen on golf courses.

$15,000: The asking price by a sports memorabilia firm for a revolver used in the suicide of Clifford Roberts. Roberts was co-founder of the Masters Golf Tournament and its chairman from 1931 until his death in 1977. Roberts killed himself next to "Ike's Pond" on the Augusta National Golf Course and is buried in a secret location somewhere on the course.

four

What's the Good Word?

olf has a lot of slang terms. Some have great stories about their origins; others don't. Here's a sampling:

Albatross You know what birdies and eagles are, but did you know that it's an *albatross* when a player plays a hole three strokes under par? These days—perhaps mindful of *The Ancient Mariner*—golfers usually call it a "double eagle."

Birdie The term for one stroke under par has been traced to one Abner H. Smith, a golfer at the Atlantic City (New Jersey) Country Club, who in either 1898 or 1903 shouted, "That's a bird of a shot!" to a fellow player when he came in one stroke under par. The story sounds a little weak to us, but who knows? Anyway, others took the avian motif and came up with eagles, double eagles, and albatrosses.

Bogey The name for going one over par has nothing to do with Humphrey Bogart. It comes from beating the "bogeyman" of the golf course. In Middle English, the term referred to a hobgoblin, bugbear, or the devil himself. A song, *The Bogey Man,* became very popular in England in 1891, and the phrase was heard often on the golf course not long after. In England, it came to mean "par," and golfers began referring to a mythical Colonel Bogey who dependably shot par. In the United States, though, bogey came to mean one stroke over par.

(A quick, golf-related tangent: *The Colonel Bogey March* was published in 1914 and later was used as the whistled theme in the 1957 movie, *The Bridge on the River Kwai.* It was written by British Lt. F. J. Ricketts under the name Kenneth Alford. The story is that Ricketts had nicknamed his golf-loving commanding officer "Colonel Bogey." On the golf course, the colonel thought it undignified to shout "Fore!" and instead whistled a loud two-note "Yoo hoo!"—in musical terms, a "descending minor third." His little musical trademark stuck in Ricketts's mind and grew into the phrase that makes up the memorable march.)

Bunke It comes from the Scottish *bunker, bunkart,* or *bonkar*—all variations of a term that means a storage hole dug into the side of a hill. It may have come originally from Old Swedish *bunke,* which is a protected part of a ship.

Burn Scottish golfers call basic water hazards "burns." Why? A burn is a spring. It's an Old English word (perhaps handed down from the German) that's still in use. Originally it meant "springing up" and could be applied to either water or fire. The water meaning faded in most parts of the world, but those across the Big Pond still use it from time to time . . . especially in the land of Robert Burns.

Caddy From French *cadet,* meaning a young man. Reportedly from the practice of Mary, Queen of Scots, who used young men from her court to carry her golf equipment.

Chip In old Scotland, *chipping* (instead of "chopping," as in England) was the word used for cutting wood with an ax.

Divot Means "a piece of turf" in Scottish.

Dolly Parton Witty (or so they thought) golfers came up with "Dolly Parton" as a slang term for a particularly hilly and uneven green.

Duffer From the Scottish *duffar* or *doofart:* "a dull, stupid person."

Fore! Best guess is that it's a shortened version of what British artillerymen shouted at infantry troops before they fired a volley over their heads: "Beware before!" meaning, "Duck!" to the people *before* them, up ahead. Over time, "Before," was shortened to "'Fore!" and "Beware" was too wordy in battle and so was dropped completely. Golfers swiped the phrase. Some claim that in 1770, John Knox, the Scottish reformer, was the first to use the term "Fore" on the golf course. This is up for debate.

Frog hairs The fine grass that borders a green on a golf course is often called "fringe" or "apron" in the United States. Across the pond, however, in Great Britain, it's also called "fringe," but it's sometimes referred to as the "collar" or "frog hairs." "Frog hairs" comes from the expression for something so fine you can hardly see it. As in, "It's as fine as frog hairs." Them limeys are an interesting lot, eh wot?

Links The term "links" comes from *hlinc,* an old Anglo-Saxon word that means "slope" or "rising ground." Early courses in Scotland were on slopes that ran down to the seas. Now the term is used more loosely as slang to mean any golf course.

Mulligan Why taking a second chance at a muffed shot is called a Mulligan nobody knows, but members of scores of old golf courses swear it came from a long-ago member named Mulligan (or in one case "Mel Egan") who was notorious for taking second and third chances when things went awry. Another legend is that it comes from "Hit 'em all again!" Or even "Mull [it over] again."

Putt Seems to come from an old spelling for *put,* as in "Put the ball in there, laddie!" However, old British meanings for the term also include a trap for fish and a cart for carrying manure.

Round Why is a game of golf called a "round"? Because courses are traditionally laid out in a loose circular pattern, bringing players at the last hole back to where they started.

Score slang Because of the number's shape, "snowman" is a slang term some witty golfer invented for a score of 8 on a hole. Likewise, "hockey stick" for a 7, and so on.

Stymie From the Scottish word meaning "not being able to see."

Tee Not from the T-shape, as you might expect, but from the Scottish word *teez*. It refers to a small pile of sand or dirt, which is what golfers teed off from before an African American dentist invented the first wooden tee. When the word traveled from Scotland, people thought that *teez* was plural, so snipped off the *z* when talking about one.

Tiger tee It's not the golf tee that Tiger Woods uses; it's the slang term applied to the very back tee.

Texas wedge If you use a putter any-where other than the green (and some peculiar folks do), you don't call it a putter. For heavens sake, no. You can call it a "Texas wedge," or nothin' a'tall. Ya hear?

five

It Takes Balls . . . and Some Clubs

The National Sporting Goods Association reports that golfers spend about $600 million every year on equipment, including clubs, bags, carts, shoes . . . and replacements for equipment destroyed in anger.

"The golfer will never settle for anything. He's too insecure. The golfer is a crazy guy. If he thinks a new ball will go a 20th of an inch longer, that's his ball."

—*Dave Lumley, marketing director, Wilson Sporting Goods*

Golfers buy more than 500 million new golf balls every year.

The first golf ball was made by the ancient Romans for the game they called *paganica*. It was made of feathers wrapped in leather. A good paganica player could drive one about 150 yards.

Scottish ball makers refined the process in the early days of "gawf." They wet a hatful of goose feathers with a mix of alum and water, squeezed them into a tight ball, and stitched them into a leather cover. The feather-and-leather ball was the state of the art for centuries. That extra compression sent the ball soaring about 180 yards.

Each "feathery" ball took about two hours to make, and so cost a lot. Worse, it tended to fall apart quickly when hit with metal clubs and became sodden and lethargic in wet weather.

Still, the feathery balls floated. As a result, in the early game of golf in Scotland, water hazards weren't so hazardous, as long as you got the ball out quickly before water seeped inside. Balls could simply be played from the surface of ponds and streams.

In 1848, the first rubber-based golf ball flew off a tee, just nine years after Charles Goodyear first vulcanized rubber. Manufacturers called it the "gutta percha," naming it after the Malaysian gum tree that gave its sap for the material (in Malay, *getah* means "gum" and *percha* means "tree").

Incidentally, gutta percha was also used for dental fillings in the eighteenth century.

Gutta percha balls revolutionized the game largely because they were much cheaper than the handmade balls they replaced. What was once a game for the fabulously wealthy became accessible to the merely affluent.

Some golf historians credit the cheapness of mass-produced gutta percha balls with spawning the golf boom of the late 1800s.

These first mass-produced golf balls weren't white. Because of the materials they were made from, they were more of a gray.

In 1899, solid gutta percha balls were replaced with "bounding billies," balls consisting of a rubber core tightly wound with rubber bands and covered with gutta percha skin.

From Pimples to Dimples

At the turn of the century, scientists began unraveling a question that had bedeviled golfers for a half-century: Why did gutta percha balls travel a distance equal to that of the feather-leather balls when new but 60 percent farther when old and beat up? After discarding several theories (including that rubber got bouncier with age), the scientists came up with a mind-boggling solution: The increased distance came from the nicks, cuts, and scratches that marred an old gutta percha ball. The spin of a nicked-up ball provided lift like that of the wings of an airplane (which hadn't been invented yet) and also made the ball fly more accurately.

Ball makers tried to incorporate this new data into the design of their balls, trying to come up with the best pattern. They tried a rough mesh design; they also tried triangle-shaped dimples, rope patterns pressed into the outer shell, circle-patterned markings, and even bumps.

In 1908, triangles and pimples gave way to the circular dimples we know now (it was the fastest and farthest-flying design). That has remained mostly unchanged for nearly a century.

In 1983, the average ball had 330 dimples. By 2001, the average ball had 415, with the range between 360 and 523 as the most popular.

Each dimple can be .01 of an inch deep.

How well do modern dimples work? Take similar balls, one with dimples and one without. If you can hit the dimpled ball 260 yards, you'll find that the same shot will send the smooth ball only 120 yards.

Ever heard of the pneumatic ball? We thought not. Made by B. F. Goodrich in 1905, the ball was filled with compressed air and hit farther than any other ball on the links. Just one, teensy-weensy problem: The ball was known to explode in the heat. The pneumatic ball died a quick and quiet death.

"**T**wo balls in the water. By God, I've got a good mind to jump in and make it four!"

—*Simon Hobday, pro golfer*

It's Not the Size of Your Balls

There is no official size for golf balls, per se—they just cannot be any bigger than 1.68 inches nor weigh more than 1.62 ounces.

For fifty-nine years, the American golf ball and the official Great Britain golf ball were two different sizes. When in 1931 the

United States Golf Association (USGA) approved a ball that measured 1.68 inches in diameter, Great Britain did not quickly follow suit. The Brits kept their ball the old standard—a maximum of 1.62 inches in diameter—until surrendering in 1990.

At one point American golfers petitioned the international rulemakers to allow them to increase the size of the hole from its standard 4 1/2 inches diameter, arguing that was only fair considering their bigger balls. They were turned down.

You might still be playing with the same ball as last year, but professional golfers switch balls every few holes, because after all those whacks, a ball tends to start getting out of round.

On a hot day, heat softens golf balls, reducing compression.

Believing folklore about golf equipment can be costly. Ask Mark Minnie of San Jose, California, who, as a seventeen-year-old, heard a radio personality say that a hot ball would travel farther than a cold one. Minnie took the information to heart and decided to put a golf ball into the family microwave. The ball exploded all over the inside of the oven.

Does the latest "miracle ball" really increase your distance? Not according to the USGA, which finds no evidence that today's golf balls travel any farther than those of twenty years ago.

Still, that doesn't stop manufacturers from trying. They've experimented with ball cores of cork, lead, ball bearings, even mercury.

A ball with a transmitter inside that allowed a player to locate it with a radio receiver was banned in the 1970s.

The USGA keeps careful tabs on the claims and specs of new equipment. Using an automated swing machine, a ball can fly no faster than 250 feet per second off the club head nor travel more than 280 yards.

The USGA swing machine, by the way, is called the Iron Byron, in honor of golfing giant Byron Nelson.

Mashies, Brassies, and Niblicks

"There are long cleeks and short cleeks, driving cleeks, lofting cleeks, putting cleeks; there are heavy irons and tight irons, driving irons, lofting irons, and sand irons. There are mashies and niblicks. In this multitude of golf clubs there is wisdom—somewhere—but it can scarcely be that all of them are necessary."

> —*Horace Hutchinson, writer and*
> *championship golfer (1890)*

In the golden age of golf, at the end of the nineteenth century, writer Robert Chambers listed the clubs that every well-equipped player had on hand:

- The *play club* for driving;
- The *mashie* or *long spoon* for getting out of roughs;
- The *short spoon* for short drives of 100 yards or less;

- The *brassie,* which was a wood with a protective brass sole;
- The *sand iron* for lofting the ball out of hazards and over stymies;
- The *cleek,* an iron for long shots; and
- The *niblick* or *track iron,* a small club with a heavy iron head made for getting the ball out of holes.

How about the rut iron? Believe it or not, it was quite useful in its heyday. The rut iron was designed especially to chip a player's ball out of a wagon-wheel rut. Fortunately for the golfer, but unfortunately for the rut iron's manufacturer, cars soon replaced wagons, and golf courses stopped allowing for through traffic.

"**W**hy am I using a new putter? Because the old one didn't float too well."

—*Craig Sandler*

The first golfers, desperate for good equipment, commissioned bow makers and carpenters to make their clubs.

Early wooden golf clubs split so easily that golfers routinely carried replacements.

As *gutties* took over where *featheries* left off, the slender, long-nosed wooden clubs (think thin, smaller hockey sticks) were simply too unstable to handle the harder balls. Club design therefore quickly changed to the more blunt, thicker and harder club style we're more familiar with today.

Golf rules set the maximum number of golf clubs in your bag at fourteen.

Persimmon wood from America is the preferred wood used for golf clubs.

A hook can be the result of using golf clubs with too much flex in their shaft.

"**I**rons" are really made from steel. So are some "woods."

The USGA ruled steel shafts illegal until 1924, when a worldwide shortage of hickory forced the issue.

"I asked my caddy for a sand wedge and he came back ten minutes later with a ham on rye."

—*Chi Chi Rodriguez*

Ever wonder why there are so many clubs? For precision of distance, at least in theory. In the hands of an average professional golfer, a driver will hit a ball about 260 yards.

3-wood: 240 yards

1-iron: 230 yards

2-iron: 220 yards

3-iron: 210 yards

4-iron: 200 yards

5-iron: 185 yards

6-iron: 175 yards

7-iron: 160 yards

8-iron: 150 yards

9-iron: 135 yards

Wedge: 120 yards

Sand wedge: 105 yards

"The most exquisitely satisfying act in the world of golf is that of throwing a club.

The full backswing, the delayed wrist action, the flowing follow-through, followed by that unique whirring sound, reminiscent only of a flock of passing starlings, is without parallel in the sport."

—*Henry Longhurst,*
British writer (?–1978)

Some of the more common (and printable) nicknames that golfers give their drivers tend to be masculine: Big Galoot, Big Dog, Killer, Thunderstick, Hammer, and the big bad name to end all big bad names, Bazooka.

The more popular nicknames for putters tend to be more feminine and personal, like the Unsinkable Molly Brown and Run-Around Sue.

"Calamity Jane" was the name of famous golfer Bobby Jones's putter. With Calamity Jane in hand, Jones managed to win all four of the big-name golf tournaments in 1930: the British Open, the British Amateur, the U.S. Amateur, and the U.S. Open.

More Bang for Your Buck: In 1996, two men patented a design for a golf club that will fire a golf ball well in excess of 280 yards without strenuous effort. The club accomplished that feat by way of a small explosive detonator in its head. Needless to say, it wasn't accepted by the USGA as legal for tournament play.

In the same year and vein, a company in San Rafael, California, brought out Peace Missile Golf Clubs, made from melted-down Soviet nuclear missiles.

Still Another Golf Innovation from 1996: A Houston man patented a telescoping device that goes inside a golf hole. When you sink your putt, the device automatically lifts your ball up high enough that you don't have to bend down to retrieve it.

Hmm . . . wonder why this one didn't catch on? The mechanized club of 1942 seemed like a good idea on the drawing board, anyway: When the player had a good swing, the club would play thunderous applause; when the golfer swung badly, the club made a loud raspberry sound. Golfers didn't like it, for some reason.

Dentists have made a lasting contribution to the game of golf. George Grant, an African American dentist, patented the first golf tee way back in 1899. It didn't fly at the time. It took another dentist, William Lowell, twenty-two years later, to make the tee a golfing success. Dr. Lowell called his version the Reddy Tee, and it, too, wasn't well received at first. There's nothing greenbacks can't solve, however. Lowell paid a huge sum—$1,500—to golf star Walter Hagen to use the tee in matches. After that, the golf tee caught on.

Another Way That Golf Resembles Base-ball: They're about the only two activities where you wear one glove, and specifically on your nondominant hand.

According to golf pros, the main reasons why professional golfers don't wear sun-glasses are because glasses slip in the hot sun and the tint alters the colors of the fair-way and green, making it hard to read the course. However, national market manager for RayBan Scott Hansberger says it's about fashion and image. As evidence, he points to the fact that sunglasses are tradi-tionally worn by standoffish movie stars, not easygoing and friendly golfers. In past celebrity pro-ams, says Hansberger, "The celebrities were all wearing sunglasses—but the pros weren't."

Tubular wicker baskets were the first golf bags, which were enough because most golfers didn't carry that many clubs or balls. Golf bags appeared during the golf boom of the late 1800s. Before that, your caddy had to lug your loose golf clubs over his shoulder or under his arm.

six

Not Our Kind of People

" **V**ery few blacks will take up golf until the requirement for plaid pants is dropped."

—Franklin Ajaye,
African American comedian

Tiger Woods' longest-lasting contribution to the game of golf? Perhaps finally shaming country clubs that still discriminate against African Americans, Jews, and other minorities.

An ugly side of the elite cult of golf: Even now, in the twenty-first century, there are golf courses in the United States where Tiger Woods would not be allowed to play because of the color of his skin. And Ladies' Professional Golf Association (LPGA) pro

Nancy Lopez, because she's a woman, would only be allowed to play during Tuesday and Friday "Ladies' Days," if at all.

Even into the 1970s, the Baltimore Country Club posted signs reading, "No Dogs, No Coloreds, No Jews." Now, at least, the all-male, all-gentile, all-Caucasian clubs usually consider it crass to actually spell this policy out, even when the exclusionary policies remain unchanged.

The venerable Burning Tree Club in Bethesda, Maryland, has never had a woman member or guest in its seventy-nine years of existence. Members' wives are allowed to enter the premises at Christmastime—but then only to visit the pro shop to buy presents for their husbands.

But progress inches forward . . . perhaps. In the 1990s, many clubs that had racial or ethnic restrictions actually written into their charters removed them (even if they remained in practice). This was after it was revealed that the site of 1990's PGA championship, Alabama's Shoal Creek course, had not even a single black member. Because of the disparity of the membership at the club, advertisers promptly pulled $2 million of TV advertising so they wouldn't be associated with exclusionary practices. In response, the PGA drafted a policy stating that no PGA event "will be held at any golf club that has membership practices or policies that discriminate on the basis of race, religion, sex, or national origin."

"**I** think it's absolutely a coincidence. We have no members from Hungary, either, and none from Lithuania or Estonia. It's a nothing. It's meaningless."

> *—Attorney and member Graham Koch trying to explain away the fact that North-wood Country Club in Dallas has never even considered a black member for membership, quoted in the* Dallas Times, *May 18, 2001*

Despite Tiger Woods, black golfers make up only 3.3 percent of all golfers—professional and amateur—a figure unchanged over the last decade.

At last count, only four golf courses in the United States are owned by African Americans, down from an all-time high of seventy, when many blacks ran their own golf courses offering otherwise excluded African American players a place to play.

When asked in 1994 why he hadn't spoken out against racism at private country clubs, Jack Nicklaus suggested African Americans weren't suited for the sport. "Blacks have different muscles that react in different ways," he said.

"Very few people will voice their opinion in public. But I guarantee you behind closed doors across the country there are people wishing to see Tiger Woods fail."

—*Bill Dickey,*
president and founder of the National
Minority Junior Golf Scholarship Association

seven

Women
Drivers

In the 1870s, the few women who wanted to play golf were required to play in full skirts, petticoats, and bustles.

These same women golfers were expected to *not* take a full swing and to stick only to ladylike strokes such as chipping and putting.

The first ladies' golf union was formed in 1893.

The first American to win an Olympic gold medal was a woman, Margaret Abbott. It happened in Paris in 1900, in the first and last year that women's golf was an Olympic event.

Most golf courses banned women from playing until the late twentieth century.

Women in Morristown, New Jersey, tired of being left out of the boys' game, formed their own golf club and built a seven-hole course. This was in 1894.

Legendary golf professionals Patty Berg and Babe Didrikson Zaharias created the Ladies' Professional Golfing Association (LPGA) in 1949.

Following the example of golf fanatic Mary, Queen of Scots, who loved the sport, there are nowadays 5.7 million female golfers—

both amateur and professional—or more than 1 in 5.

Women make up 39 percent of beginning golfers.

However, half of all beginning women quit the game within a year.

In 1993, the Ladies' Pro Golf Association realized it was necessary to arrange for traveling day care for the mothers on the pro tour, most of whom didn't make nearly enough to hire a nanny.

They still don't. Women pros make a small fraction of what men pros make. For example, as of July 30, 2001, the top-ranking man in the PGA earned $4,456,311 for the year; the top-ranked woman had earned 42 percent of that, or $1,876,853. Things get much worse for women the further they are from the top: The 150th-ranked man in the PGA made $184,613; the 150th-ranked woman, $21,919—less than 12 percent of his earnings.

The first LPGA member who made $1 million in career earnings was Kathy Whitworth, and that didn't happen until 1981.

"Live...Laugh...GOLF!"

—Kathryn Schaefer Plaum

leight

Golf Pros . . . and Cons

GEO. MORROW.

Golf great Bobby Jones won tournament after tournament, including the British Open three times and the U.S. Open four times. How much money did Jones win in his sterling career? $0. He was the greatest amateur player of all time (his career culminating in the 1930s), and he never turned pro.

Bobby Jones, the golfer, is not the same guy as Robert Trent Jones, the golf course designer.

For that matter, there are two Robert Trent Joneses—Senior and Junior, both golf course designers. Senior died in 2000; Junior is, last time we checked, still going strong.

Chi Chi Rodriguez's real first name is Juan. (And no, this is not the time to tell the joke about the golf gun that shoots a hole in Juan.)

Tiger Woods was the youngest U.S. Amateur Champion ever.

Nancy Lopez won the New Mexico Amateur in 1969 . . . at the age of twelve.

Lee Way

Lee Trevino's father was a professional grave digger.

As a kid, Lee Trevino used to bet golfers on the local course that he could beat them by playing with a Dr. Pepper bottle that had a stick taped to it. He often won.

Trevino flees from the fairways whenever rain begins to come down. There's good reason for his phobia: he's been hit by lightning. He admits, "When God wants to play through, I let him play through."

Pro golfing's first millionaires were Jack Nicklaus, Arnold Palmer, and Gary Player.

When you think of professional golf winners, you think big bucks, right? That's not always been the case. During World War II, the total PGA Tour purse was a mere $150,000. Winners had to divide that sum—not in cash, but in the form of war bonds.

Not all pro golfers rake it in when they take on corporate sponsors. Howard Twitty, for example, signed a deal in 1977 with Burger King that didn't pay him a cent. In exchange for sporting their logo on his golf bag, they paid him in Whoppers. A total of 500 of them, to be exact.

Remember the good old days when doctors would take chickens and other essentials in exchange for their services? Well take a gander at some of the more odd prize winnings of these pro golfers:

- Oklahoma City University basketball coach Abe Lemons won a bottle of Geritol at the Golf and Country Club Tournament in Frederick, Oklahoma.

- Willie Park won a Moroccan leather belt for his victory in the 1860 British Open.

- Lee Trevino won a dagger inlaid with jewels from the Moroccan Grand Prix Pro-Am.

- Gene Littler was paid in silver dollars at the 1955 Las Vegas Tournament of Champions.

- Ian Baker-Finch won a cow in the 1988 Bridgestone/Aso (Japan) Open. He sold the cow back for $5,000.
- Bobby Jones never won a dime. He was an amateur for his entire professional career. However, he was given a gun for winning his division in the 1933 Savannah Open.

"**Y**ou know you're on the Senior Tour when your back goes out more than you do."

—*Bob Bruce*

More professional golfers are born in California than any other state, but more live in Florida.

Here are a few of our favorite golfer's nicknames:

- Joanne "Big Momma" Carner: Carner was a huge hitter, anywhere on the links.

- Fred "Boom Boom" Couples: The name speaks of his long and hard drives.

- David "Rock" Duval: When asked, Duval, laughing, says someone in college gave it to him "for one reason or another." (Duval is known for his standoffish, unemotional, and rock-solid demeanor.)

- Mildred "Babe" Didrikson: She earned her moniker during her baseball years when fans and commentators compared her hitting to the great Babe Ruth's.

- Ernie "The Big Easy" Els: He's tall and easygoing. He makes the game look like it's a walk in the park.

- Lora "Baby Faced Killer" Fairclough: Dubbed this by the late Bill Johnson when Fairclough was just a babe at fifteen years of age.

- Sergio "El Niño" Garcia: Supposedly young Sergio got this name from the Spanish, meaning "The Boy." Perhaps there's a double meaning, too, with the very stormy weather patterns—El Niño—that crop up every few years and Garcio's talent for taking a course by storm.

- Sophie "Soffan" Gustafson: Endearingly dubbed "Soph" or "Soffan" by her handball coach.

- Tim "Lumpy" Herron: When he was a teenager, some guys at his place of work nicknamed him Lumpy because of his physique.

- Ben "The Iceman" Hogan: The nickname gave a hint to Hogan's demeanor. Nothing phased him. It's said that the Scottish added a "Wee" to Hogan's moniker.

- Kim "(Ultra) Super Peanut" Mi-Hyun: At 5-foot-1-inch, Korean native Kim was named this because of her small stature, yet she packs a mighty punch on the golf course.

- Nancy "Slowpez" Lopez: Not meant politely, Lopez earned the name for her slowness on the course. In the early '90s, *Sports Illustrated* reported that she had her caddy line up all of her shots prior to playing them, without exception.

- Cary "Doc" Middlecoff: Because he once trained to be a dentist.

- "Lord Byron" Nelson: "Lord of the Links" was the reference here because Nelson was truly one of the greats in the game of golf. The reference is also to the great nineteenth-century poet Lord Byron.

- Jack "The Golden Bear" Nicklaus: Being blond and sturdy earned Nicklaus his familiar title.

- Greg "The Great White Shark" Norman: Norman earned his nickname because he talked a lot of enjoying deep-sea fishing. His very white-blond appearance and his Australian accent also helped solidify the name.

- Corey "Bulldog" Pavin: Given the name by fellow PGA player Mark O'Meara because of Pavin's persistence (like a bulldog that won't let go of your pants leg). Commentators and fans picked up on it, and it stuck.

- Marilynn "Miss Personality" Smith: Smith was always full of smiles and had an outgoing personality.

- Craig "The Walrus" Stadler: From his thick build and walrus-like mustache.

- Louise "Miss Sluggs" Suggs: Bob Hope dubbed her thus because of her series of wins throughout her career.

- Lee "Supermex" Trevino: Refers to his Mexican American heritage.

- Eldrick "Tiger" Woods: His father gave him his nickname when he was a boy, after a Vietnamese soldier whom Woods Sr. befriended named Nguyen "Tiger" Phong.

Some of the better known professional odd shots include:

- Sam Snead's ball landing in the men's bathroom of the Cleveland Open

- Bobby Jones's ball coming to rest in an abandoned shoe that was inside a parked wheelbarrow
- Hale Irwin's ball that lodged in the bra of a spectator at the Sea Pines Heritage Classic
- Cary Middlecoff's ball landing in a spectator's pocket. In the latter case, the befuddled spectator panicked and threw the ball into the rough, costing Middlecoff a double bogey on the hole.

Hot shots David Duval, Al Geiberger, and Chip Beck are the only three PGA players to ever officially score a 59 on an eighteen-hole course.

Occupational Hazards

The 1957 Bing Crosby National Pro-Am was played on the surf-and-turf golf course, Pebble Beach. On the ninth hole, overlooking an ocean vista, Tony Lema hit a good shot and jumped for joy. Unfortunately, he was close to the cliffs and ended up tumbling down a steep embankment, suffering bruises but no breaks. Lema didn't have the same good luck on a golf course nine years later, when his private plane crashed into a water hazard in Lansing, Illinois, killing him.

At the 1934 U.S. Open, Bobby Cruick-shank got a reminder of why they're called "clubs." He tossed his golf club into the air in celebration when on the eleventh hole his golf ball miraculously skipped across a water hazard to the other side. Unfortunately, the laws of gravity carry a heavy penalty—the club came down and struck him on the head, knocking him unconscious. Cruickshank played the rest of the round semidazed, coming in third with a 76.

Gary Player had the worst luck with admirers. Not only did a fan shaking his hand at the 1962 Masters sprain it and cost him the tournament, but also in 1964, during the U.S. Open, Player was accidentally shoved into the water by autograph seekers.

In 1977, as a publicity stunt, Arnold Palmer hit a sleeve of golf balls off the Eiffel Tower. As far as we know, no French person was hurt or killed in the making of this stunt.

Greg Norman accidentally hit a rock during a swing of his club at the U.S. Open at Brookline, Massachusetts, in 1988. The effects were gruesome: he badly tore a tendon in his wrist, placing him in the hospital and out of commission for months.

What A Babe!

You may know Babe Didrikson Zaharias as the woman who helped found the Ladies' Professional Golf Association. However, her sports career was as diverse as a career could be. Before she was a golfer, she was an all-around track-and-field superstar. She held world records in the following: long jump, 80-meter hurdles, javelin, and high jump. In 1932, she won two gold medals at the Summer Olympics. She also was an excellent basketball player, swimmer, marksman, cyclist, diver, softball player, and skater. Where else could she go but up? Babe went on to become a Hall of Famer in the golf world, winning three separate U.S. Open championships—in 1948, 1950, and 1954—not to mention twenty-eight other tournament wins of her career.

Babe Didrikson was set up to play an exhibition game in 1938 Los Angeles to show off her hard drives to the public. Paired with a 250-pound wrestler named George "The Crying Greek from Cripple Creek" Zaharias, Didrikson's life was about to change. When walking the course, somewhere around the seventh hole, Babe realized her partner was staring intently at her. She challenged, "What are you looking at?" George replied, "I'm looking at you. You're my kind of girl." To which Babe replied, "You're my kind of guy." George and Babe were married the following year. They were loving and close; virtually inseparable for the next eighteen years, until Babe's death from cancer in 1956.

"**I**t's not enough just to swing at the ball; you've got to loosen your girdle and really let the ball have it."

—Babe Didrikson

Too Good of a Sweep: The 1956 Tasmanian Open had an interesting winners' circle. The winner was a guy named Peter Toogood. His dad, Alfred Toogood, came in second. His brother John Toogood, finished third.

Chick Evans Jr. competed in U.S. Amateur Championships in all of the fifty states, the only golfer to ever accomplish this feat. He began by winning his first U.S. Amateur Championship in 1907 and played in his last one in 1962. Evans was seventy-two when he attained his goal.

Tiger, Tiger, Burning Bright

Boy Wonder: You may think you were introduced to Eldrick "Tiger" Woods when he stormed the amateur circuit not too many years ago. However, a whole audience of Americans first saw him sitting on Fran Tarkenton's lap two decades ago.

Woods was featured on the TV show *That's Incredible* when he was just five years old—the same year he received his first set of golf clubs. He drove whiffle balls over and over again to the *Wow*'s of audience members. Tiger had also wowed fellow golfers that year by hitting in the 90s on an eighteen-hole course his first time playing.

As the story goes, Tiger Woods, as a wee tot, once out-putted a bunch of older junior golfers and won a pocket full of quarters. His father reprimanded him, as Woods Sr. was strictly against gambling. He told Tiger that he didn't want him coming home with any more quarters in his pockets. The next time out, Tiger came back with his pockets filled with dollar bills instead.

Tiger Woods at eighteen was the youngest U.S. Amateur Champion ever.

While playing on the Stanford golf team, "Tiger" picked up a new nickname, according to *Sports Illustrated* (July 13, 2000). The boys called him "Urkel" after the accordion-playing African American nerd on TV's *Family Matters*.

Have you seen the cute little tiger club cover that Tiger Woods carries around on one of his drivers? That was a handmade gift from his mother, Kultida (or "Tida"). Inside, an inscription in Thai reads, "Love, from Mom."

Tiger Woods's mother also believes that red is a "power color" for her son—sort of a spiritual thing, we guess. This is why he wears a red shirt on his last day of tournament play.

Everyone knows Tiger Woods, but do you remember some of these other African American players?

- Dewey Brown played during the segregation days; however, no one knew he was black, so he was technically the first African American to be a member of the PGA. He was kicked out when it was discovered he was not technically Caucasian.

- African American golfer Bill Spiller protested the racist PGA Caucasian clause in 1952 by delaying the start of the San Diego Open.

- Bill Wright was the first black player to win a tournament that was sponsored by the United States Golf Association.

- The first black player to win a tournament on the PGA Tour was Charlie Sifford.

- Pete Brown was the first black person to win a PGA event.

- Lee Elder was the first African American to play in the Masters Tournament.

Talk the Talk: If you want to sound like a professional on the golf course, pro golfer Bob Heintz recommends this: "Don't ask a veteran if he's playing in the AT&T Pebble

Beach National Pro-Am. You just say, "So, are you gonna play Pebble this year?" Heintz says he doesn't know why some shortened tournament names identify the city they're played in while others are taken from the title or the sponsor. But he's quick to remind, "The key is to avoid saying the entire name."

Leo Diegel often won bets with fellow golfers by wagering that he could shoot a 75 or under while playing on just one leg.

Thundering Bolt

Tommy Bolt, professional golf champion in the '50s, was notorious for throwing his clubs when he got angry. Because of his temper, he earned the nickname "Terrible" Tommy Bolt. His club throwing also instigated a new rule in the PGA: No throwing clubs. It's called the "Tommy Bolt Rule" and penalizes a player for throwing any club during play.

The day after the "Tommy Bolt Rule" passed, Bolt became the first golfer to break it. It wasn't that he threw his club in anger, he explained, he just didn't want to see anybody else be the first to break "his" rule.

He must've been the golf team captain at ol' P.U. In the 1959 Memphis Invitational Open, Tommy Bolt was fined heavily for unsportsmanlike conduct. Not for yelling or cursing (which wasn't unusual with Bolt, mind you), but for breaking wind while a fellow player was putting.

nine

A Penalty for Your Thoughts

It's against the rules of golf to either ask for advice or give it. The penalty is one stroke added to your score. (Partners and caddies are specifically exempted from this rule.) Despite this prohibition, here are some gems of advice, some which are well worth the penalty stroke.

"Take it easy and lazily, because the golf ball isn't going to run away from you while you're swinging."

—*Sam Snead*

"You've just got one problem. You stand too close to the ball after you've hit it."

—*Sam Snead*

"**B**eing left-handed is a big advantage: No one knows enough about your swing to mess you up with advice."

—*Bob Charles*

"**N**ever bet with anyone you meet on the first tee who has a deep suntan, a one iron in his bag and squinty eyes."

—*Dave Marr*

"**L**ay off for three weeks, and then quit for good."

—*Sam Snead*

"**I**f you are going to throw a club, it is important to throw it ahead of you, down the fairway, so you don't have to waste energy going back to pick it up."

—*Tommy Bolt*

"Never break your putter and driver in the same match, or you're dead."

—*Tommy Bolt*

"The man who can putt is a match for anyone."

—*Willie Park Jr., British Open Champion in 1887 and 1889*

"Ninety percent of putts that are short don't go in."

—*Yogi Berra*

"Through years of experience, I have found that air offers less resistance than dirt."

—Jack Nicklaus

"The ideal build for a golfer would be strong hands, big forearms, thin neck, big thighs, and a flat chest. He'd look like Popeye."

—Gary Player

"Golf courses use toxic pesticides and herbicides. Don't be cleaning the ball with your tongue or licking your fingers, and don't play barefoot. After a round, wash your hands."

—Frank Coffey

"Your financial cost can best be figured out when you realize that if you were to devote the same time and energy to business instead of golf, you would be a millionaire in approximately six weeks."

—*Buddy Hackett*

"**I** have a tip that will take five strokes off anyone's game. It's called an eraser."

—*Arnold Palmer*

"**O**ne of the advantages bowling has over golf is that you seldom lose a bowling ball."

—*Don Carter, bowling pro*

"**T**he reason the pro tells you to keep your head down is so you can't see him laughing."

—*Phyllis Diller*

"**I** found out that all the important lessons of life are contained in the three rules for achieving a perfect golf swing. 1.Keep your head down. 2. Follow through. 3. Be born with money."

—*P. J. O'Rourke*

"The more I practice, the luckier I get."
—*Gary Player*

"What goes up must come down. But don't expect it to come down where you can find it."

—*Lily Tomlin*

"You make a lot of money in this game. Just ask my ex-wives. Both of them are so rich that neither of their husbands work."

—*Lee Trevino*

ten

From the Greens to the Court

Al Capone always carried a gun in his bag when he went golfing. While playing at Burnham Woods Golf Course near Chicago, the gun went off accidentally, shooting a "hole in one" . . . of Scarface's feet.

Forty-six years later, Ohio golfer Bob Russell managed to get a similar hole in one (leg, in his case) when he divotted a little too deeply and set off a bullet that had somehow gotten buried under the turf.

But Officer, We Were Only Working on Our Grip: In 1993, four men, including an elementary school teacher, were arrested on a fairway at a golf course in Little Rock,

Arkansas. The members of the foursome were standing in a circle masturbating.

In 1994, Californian Tom Stafford's drive went wide and the ball ricocheted off a steel pole, hitting him in the head. He sued the golf course in Mission Viejo for not preventing that possibility and won $8,500.

When Sporting Goods Become Sporting *Bads:* In 1995, a bicyclist was robbed of $75 by three youths after they threw a golf ball at him, knocking him off his bicycle.

In 1995, the Maine Supreme Court upheld a judgment against the Fort Kent Golf

Course. Jeannine Pelletier was awarded $40,000 because a golf ball she hit rebounded off a train track and hit her in the face.

In 1996, Diana Nagy sued the manufacturer of a golf cart, claiming they should've included doors and seat belts. Her husband had died after falling out of one after he'd been drinking at the Berry Hills Country Club in Charleston, West Virginia. Mrs. Nagy's son was driving the cart at the time, so she sued him, too.

In 1997, Dale Larson won a $41,000 lawsuit against a golf course in Wausau, Wisconsin, after he slipped while wearing his golf spikes and fell onto his face, requiring major dental work. Larson argued that he wouldn't have lost his footing if the path had been concrete instead of brick, and a jury agreed, ruling that the golf course was 51 percent responsible for his injuries. They deemed Larson only 49 percent responsible, despite having consumed thirteen drinks that evening. (Ninety minutes after his accident, Larson's blood alcohol level measured .28.)

eleven

Fore-Footed Friends

*S*heep don't make the best company. Some experts believe it was lonely shepherds who invented golf. Using their long staffs, they batted around stones or other small, rolling objects to keep them occupied during their long watches.

Fowl Ball: Many flocks of geese have discovered that migrating isn't what it's cracked up to be. They're staying put, "migrating" just a few miles before settling in on parks and golf courses for the winter, living a life of leisure surrounded by water and green fields, not worrying about any hazards beyond the occasional bad slice. Golf course managers have tried a number of solutions from sheep dogs to scarecrows, without that much effect.

At least the geese don't steal the balls. Golfers in Australia report that crows and currawongs (an indigenous black bird) swoop down and steal balls. When one bird's nest was blasted with a water cannon, 40–50 golf balls came raining down.

In 1994, a farmer in Germany sued the owner of a golf course. The farmer had been complaining that errant golfers had been hooking balls into his field for years. After the mysterious death of one cow, a veterinarian discovered a golf ball lodged in its throat. Further investigation revealed that thirty of his cows had developed the habit of swallowing golf balls and that they collectively had a total of 2,000 balls lodged in their stomachs.

At the Talamore Golf Course in Southern Pines, North Carolina, you have the option of renting an old-fashioned golf cart for $20 . . . or a llama caddy for $100 (free llama T-shirt and hat included).

How's this for a hole-in-one? In 1981, on a par 3 hole at Mountain View (California) Golf Course, amateur Ted Barnhouse, hit a wayward ball over a fence into a cow pasture. The ball bounced off a grazing cow's head and ricocheted off a lawn mower onto the green, where it bounced off the flag and into the hole.

The cow's revenge? A stampeding herd of about fifty cows invaded the eighteenth hole of the 1984 St. Andrews Trophy, menacing several golfers in their path. Cattleclysm was avoided when the stampede was diverted by officials and golfers shouting and waving 8-irons.

Once while playing in a golf tournament abroad, Sam Snead was attacked by an ostrich. The birdie bit him on the hand, rendering him out of commission for two weeks.

On a golf course in Natal, South Africa, Molly Whitaker was about to hit a shot from a bunker when a monkey leaped from a tree and wrapped his arms around her neck. Her caddie chased it away, and the game continued.

twelve

Are You a Player?

olf picks up 1.5 million to 3 million new players every year. The bad news is it loses about an equal number each year due to death, injury, or disinterest.

According to the National Golf Foundation (NGF), "Today's typical golfer is male, forty-three years old, has an average household income of $61,000, and plays sixteen rounds per year."

Twenty-five percent of all U.S. golfers are older than fifty. They play an average of thirty-six rounds per year.

About 15 percent of all golfers live in golf communities. Another 3 percent own residences or vacation homes on golf courses.

As of 2001, the average fee paid per game of golf was $36.

Only 38 percent of golfers are from households headed by blue-collar or clerical workers.

According to the National Golf Foundation, 22 percent of golfers say they regularly score better than 90. This breaks down to 25 percent of all male golfers who say they do and 7 percent of the women.

Six percent of all male golfers say they regularly break 80; 1 percent of all female golfers make that claim.

The average eighteen-hole golf score for all golfers is like the average IQ—it's 100.

The average golf score for men is 97; for women, 114.

According to the NGF, there are more than 18 million golfers in the United States.

The *New York Times* puts the number at 25 million.

The Northern Texas Golf Association fixes the number at 26.5 million, or roughly 12 percent of the population.

Some weekends it seems like all of them are on the course ahead of you.

A Round of Ice Golf, Anyone? There are more golfers per capita in Minneapolis, Minnesota, than in any other city in the United States.

A *Washington Post* poll reportedly found that 70 percent of Fortune 500 CEOs regularly did business on the golf course.

"**G**eneral Motors is basically run out of the Bloomfield Hills Country Club," according to Dave Richards, a golf pro from that affluent Michigan suburb.

In the 1990s, the *New York Times* published a study demonstrating a positive correlation between a CEO's golf handicap and his or her company's performance.

Seventeen percent of sales reps who play golf with clients admitted in a Gallup Poll that they routinely let their clients win.

According to a company called Business Golf Strategies, which teaches companies how to sell on the golf course, the first four holes are for building rapport. Holes five through fifteen are for talking business. After that, stop discussing business and make sure your customer is enjoying the game...then go in for the kill while drinking at the "nineteenth hole."

"Who's Your Caddy!"

The Evans Scholarships were started by Charles "Chick" Evans, who learned to play golf while a caddy. He went on to become, in 1916, the first golfer ever to win both the U.S. Amateur and U.S. Open championships in the same year. Because Evans chose to preserve his amateur status, he directed that any money he won from golf be put into a scholarship fund for those who serve by carrying and waiting.

The Evans Scholarships provide $7 million every year to "deserving caddies" attending college in the Midwest.

"Man blames fate for other accidents, but feels personally responsible for a hole-in-one."

—*Martha Beckman, humor writer*

The oldest man to "shoot his age" was a 103-year-old from Canada who scored, well, 103.

Has anybody scored two holes-in-one in a row? It's not impossible—at least twenty people have done exactly that.

"I'm hitting the woods just great. But I'm having a terrible time getting out of them."
— *Harry Toscano*

Southeast Asia is the fastest growing golf market in the world.

In 1963, a man named Floyd Satterlee Rood decided to drive across America. "Drive," that is, in the sense of hitting a golf ball from coast to coast. He started at the water hazard we call the Pacific Ocean on September 14, 1963, and by October 3, 1964, had made it to the Atlantic. He took 114,737 strokes to cover the 3,397.7 miles and lost 3,511 balls along the way.

We'd Give Our Right Arms to Join This Club: The Society of One-Armed Golfers, located at 11 Campbell Place, Torrance, Glasgow G64 4HR "organise week-long championships, weekend and day events for golfers using only one hand. Communication between members is by newsletter, normally three per year."

A name can make or break a tournament. Consider these now-defunct tourneys: The Hardscrabble Open, The Girl Talk Classic, The Gasparilla Open, The Rubber City Open, and our all-time favorite has-been golf competition (drum roll, please) ... The Iron Lung Open.

Angelo Spagnolo is the worst avid golfer. No, really. When *Golf Digest* sponsored a tournament called The Worst Avid Golfer Tournament, he won, hands down. Some of Spagnolo's finest moments during the championship included a 66 on a par 3 and an amassed 124 penalty strokes for his foursome during the round. His score on the eighteen-hole course was 257.

A mere heart attack was not enough to keep Dr. Pedro Brugado from winning a Brussels amateur golf tournament in 1996. A cardiologist, ironically, Brugado was in the lead when he suffered a heart attack on the final round. An opponent who was also a physician revived Brugado and had him rushed to a hospital. He was released 90 minutes later to finish the hole and win the tournament.

Lucky break or act of God? You decide. In 1956, when Morton Shapiro hit his ball up to the lip of the fifth hole of the Indian Springs Country Club in New Jersey, a ground tremor gently shook the earth, sending his balancing ball into the cup for a hole-in-one.

Your Ace and a Hole in the Ground

Scott Statler hit a hole-in-one on July 30, 1962, at the seventh hole of Statler's Par 3 Golf Course in Greensburg, Pennsylvania. He was all of four years old.

Harold Hoyt Stilson Sr., holds the record for the oldest person to ever score a hole-in-one. He swung to greatness at the ripe old age of 101 on the 16th hole at Deerfield Country Club in Florida, on May 16, 2001. Stilson died less than a year later on February 2, 2002.

In 1986, at the age of ninety-five, Erna Ross was the oldest woman to hit a hole-in-one. It was the seventeenth hole of the Everglades Golf Club in Palm Beach, Florida.

Brittny Andreas accomplished quite a feat: At the age of six, Brittny was the youngest girl to ever hit a hole-in-one. It happened on the Jimmy Clay Golf Course in Austin, Texas, in 1991.

thirteen

Life According to Golf

"The arc of your swing doesn't have a thing to do with the size of your heart."

—Carol Mann, Golf Hall of Famer

"Ambition is a grievous fault . . . and grievously doth the duffer pay."

—William Shakespeare

"One of the very important attractions of golf is that it provides a wide and varied assortment of topics for conversation."

—Bobby Jones

"The place of the father in the modern suburban family is a very small one, particularly if he plays golf."

—Bernard Russell

"Golf giveth and golf taketh away, but it taketh away a hell of a lot more than it giveth."

—*Simon Hobday*

"The golf swing is like sex: You can't be thinking of the mechanics of the act while you're doing it."

—*Dave Hill*

"Golf is second only to Christianity, and is its greatest ally in the development of the highest standard of American manhood and womanhood."

—*Rev. Dr. Paul Arnold Peterson*

"**T**hey say that golf
is a lot like life,
but don't believe them.
Golf is a lot more
complicated than that."

—*Gardner Dickinson,*
a founder of the Senior PGA Tour

"**I**f there is any larceny in man, golf will bring it out."

—*Unknown golf lover*

"**I**f you think it's hard to meet new people, try picking up the wrong golf ball."

—*Jack Lemmon*

"**A**s you walk down the fairway of life you must smell the roses, for you only get to play one round."

—*Ben Hogan*

"**I**n golf as in life, it's the follow through that makes the difference."

—*Edward Zorn, commentator*

"There are three things as unfathomable as they are fascinating to the masculine mind: metaphysics, golf, and the feminine heart."

—Arnold Haultain

"The beauty of golf stems from the fact that success, as well as failure, comes from within."

—Tom Watson

"I never really dreamed of making many putts. Maybe that's why I haven't made many."

—Calvin Peete, golfer

"Golf is a game of inches. The most important are those between the ears."

—*Arnold Palmer*

"The worst club in my bag is my brain."

—*Chris Perry, golfer*

"The fun you get from golf is in direct ratio to the effort you don't put into it."

—*Bob Allen*

"Most golfers prepare for disaster. A good golfer prepares for success."

—*Bob Toski, one of the world's leading golf instructors*

"**A** lot of guys who have never choked have never been in the position to do so."

—*Tom Watson*

"**I**f you want to beat someone out on the golf course, just get him mad."

—*Dave Williams, "Father of College Golf"*

"**R**eal golfers don't cry when they line up their fourth putt."

—*Unknown*

"**G**olf is 90 percent mental and 10 percent mental."

—*Thomas Mulligan*

"Some of us worship in churches, some in synagogues, some on golf courses."

—*Adlai Stevenson*

"Of all the hazards, fear is the worst."

—*Sam Snead*

"The uglier a man's legs are, the better he plays golf. It's almost a law."

—*H. G. Wells*

"The mind messes up more shots than the body."

—*Tommy Bolt*

"**I**t matters not whether you win or lose; what matters is whether I win or lose."

—*Darin Weinberg, golf lover*

fourteen

A Course Is a Course, Of Course, Of Course

As of summer 2001, the United States had 16,743 golf courses.

Florida is the state with the most golf courses, followed by California, Michigan, Texas, and New York.

At last count, Myrtle Beach in South Carolina has 123 of them, located along the "Grand Strand," a 60-mile stretch of traffic-clogged beach highway.

About 400 new golf courses open each year in the United States.

Golf courses now cover about as much of America as the states of Delaware and Rhode Island combined.

Another way of looking at that is that the country has one golf hole for every 139 people.

The average nine-hole course covers about 65 acres; the average eighteen-hole course, about 150.

"If you try to fight the course, it will beat you."

—*Lou Graham*

Fighting the course might make some sense, though, if a name is any indication. Here are some names of actual golf courses we'd suggest watching out for:

- Bloody Point Club (Dafuskie Island, South Carolina)
- Nutcracker Golf Club (Granbury, Texas)
- Dub's Dread Golf Club (Lawrence, Kansas)
- Predator Ridge Golf Resort (Vernon, British Columbia)

These golf courses may not sound as scary, but we'd still give 'em a pass:

- Bull Valley Golf Club (Woodstock, Illinois)

- Sunken Meadow State Park Golf Club (Kings Park, New York)
- Potholes Golf and Camping (Othello, Washington)
- Double Dam Golf Club (Claysville, Pennsylvania)
- Broken Woods Golf Club (Coral Springs, Florida)

"**I** use the word 'bunker'; meaning a pit in which the soil has been exposed and the area covered with sand. I regard the term 'sand trap' as an unacceptable Americanization. Its use annoys me almost as much as hearing a golf club called a 'stick.' Earthworks, mounds, and the like, without sand, are not 'bunkers.'"

—Bobby Jones (golf course designer)
being grouchy

According to the golf industry, a golf course needs about 40,000 paid rounds of golf each year to make a profit.

Want your own high-end golf course designed by a top course designer? Expect to pay about $7 million dollars to build it.

Otherwise, the rule of thumb is that a golf course will cost from $200,000 to $400,000 per hole.

It wasn't always this way. In the good old days of golfing—a century or two ago—course designers played the terrain as it laid, and they saw their job as simply figuring out the best use of the available features that came with the land. They would pace out the available ground, marking tees and greens with colored stakes. Laying out an eighteen-hole course wouldn't usually take more than a day or two.

Old Tom Morris, legendary golfer and course designer from St. Andrews, Scotland, was one of the leading golf course architects in the 1800s. He charged one English pound a day, plus his expenses, to design a course . . . and he seldom took more than two days.

You'd think that all that greenery would be a good addition to the environment. Unfortunately not. To make a golf course, designers uproot the native plants and animals living there and replace them with huge expanses of turf.

To keep all that grass green, an average golf course uses about one million gallons of water a day, or the equivalent of a small town's total water usage.

The average golf course uses a staggering 18 pounds of pesticides per acre. (A crop of soybeans, in contrast, typically uses only about a pound of chemicals per acre.)

In 2000, the Anarchist Golfing Association vandalized genetically altered grass that was designed to improve putting greens, causing $300,000 in damage. "Grass, like industrial culture, is invasive," charged an e-mail taking responsibility that was sent anonymously from a library in Eugene, Oregon.

The Greens Party

In developing countries, the creation of golf courses for rich foreigners has become a significant political issue. A group calling itself the Global Anti-Golf Movement was formed to work against building golf courses.

"The transformation of golf memberships into a saleable commodity has resulted in widespread speculation and dubious practices," says the Global Anti-Golf Movement Manifesto. "In many countries golf course/resort development is in reality often a hit-and-run business. . . . The bulk of the foreign exchange earned from golf courses and golf tourism does not stay in the local economy but are reaped by a few business people."

The GAGM Manifesto goes on: "These landscaped foreign systems create stress on local water supplies and soil, at the same time being highly vulnerable to disease and pest attacks. . . . The construction of golf courses in scenic natural sites, such as forest areas and coral islands, also results in the destruction of biodiversity. . . . The environmental impacts include water depletion and toxic contamination of the soil, underground and surface water, and the air. This in turn leads to health problems for local communities, populations down-stream and even golfers, caddies, and chemical sprayers at golf courses."

GAGM has designated April 29 as World No-Golf Day. Workers of the world, put down your putters—you have nothing to lose but your slice.

In the 1930s, during what was called the "rinky-dink golf" craze, there were about 50,000 miniature golf courses, including about 3,000 in the "Tom Thumb Golf" chain.

On a cliff hanging over the Pacific Ocean, the sixteenth hole on Cypress Point is a killer. It's the place where Groucho Marx quit golf. Marx loved golf, but one day while playing against TV host Ed Sullivan, he hit five tee shots into the ocean. Rather than tee up again, he calmly picked up his golf bag, carried it to the edge of the cliff, and tossed it into the ocean. Afterward, he explained: "It's not that I'm a poor loser, but I figured if I couldn't beat a fellow with no neck, I've got to be the world's worst golfer and I have no right to be on a course at all."

Pebble Beach has the highest greens fees in the United States: $275 per round.

The Pebble Beach course was founded by Samuel Morse, whose other claim to fame was that he was the nephew of the guy who invented the telegraph.

The world's largest sand bunker, called Hell's Half Acre, at Pine Valley in Clementon, New Jersey, extends 100 yards along the hole.

The highest golf course in the world is the Tuctu Golf Club in Morococha in Peru—it's 14,335 feet above sea level.

The longest single hole on a golf course is the sixth at the Koolan Island course in

Australia, which measures 948 yards and is a par 7 hole.

How do greenskeepers measure the speed of a green? They use a stimpmeter, which is essentially a slanted grooved bar. They roll the ball down the bar and measure its distance. They do that several times from several different directions and average the results.

Believe it or not, a golf company purposely developed a golf ball that would travel only half the distance of normal golf balls—like 140 yards down the fairway. In a game where long drives are usually the ultimate goal, this might seem strange. However, when Jack Nicklaus and his company wanted to build a course on the small Caribbean island of Grand Cayman, he couldn't find enough land for a low enough price to build a full-size course. He decided to make it a smaller scale—about 4,000 yards—and make a rule that only short-range balls could be used. Nicklaus dubbed the new variation "Cayman Golf," and since then, other half-size courses have been built.

Where's the longest golf course in the world? In Bolton, Massachusetts. The International Golf Club sports an 8,325 yard, par 77 course. It has the largest green in the world, as well—the one on the fifth hole measures 28,000 square feet.

Quick, Caddy, a Sand Wedge! In 1931, Bayly MacArthur was playing in New South Wales, Australia, and hit his ball into what he thought was a bunker. When he stepped into it, however, it turned out to be quicksand. Other golfers heard his cry and pulled MacArthur out.

Uganda's Jinja Golf Course has a couple of interesting additions to the usual golf rules that may not be encountered anywhere else in the world. For instance, if a ball lands near a crocodile and it's deemed unsafe to play it, you may drop another ball. Also, if your ball lands in a hippopotamus footprint, you may lift and drop the ball without incurring penalty. (Don't try invoking these rules at St. Andrews, however—they just won't fly.)

Golfers in Japan are either very lucky or very confused—most courses there have two greens for each hole. There's a good reason for this, actually. Because of climate and weather in that country, one green on each hole is grown with a vigorous, tough native grass that stays playable all year round. The other green is resodded seasonally with the traditional golfer's bent grass, which doesn't survive well in Japan's climate.

"If your ball lands within a club length of a rattlesnake, you are allowed to move your ball," states a sign of local rules at the Glen Canyon golf course in Arizona.

The Los Angeles Country Club, built in 1897, was originally a dump . . . literally! Built on an active garbage dump, it originally used tin cans as holes and various piles of garbage as hazards. In its present incarnation, without the cans and old tires, it's considered to be one of the finest courses in the nation and is extremely hard to get in to.

Looking for a little tournament variety? How about this: Every August, Greenland plays host to an odd tournament indeed. Actually, it's put on by the Thule Army Base located at the base of Mount Dundas. The mountain is a steep 720-foot climb that participants scale prior to beginning the rocky, nine-hole, par 36 tourney. Hosts spray paint circles of rocks green on the course, and players must tote—along with their one allotted club and two golf balls—a square of carpet to putt from. The players in the annual tournament receive this certificate of participation:

Let it be know and made a matter of record that: on (date), (your name here) did with reckless abandon and total disregard for life and limb, take golf club in hand and scale the treacherous heights of Mt. Dundas and with a dazzling display of hooks, slices, bad bounces, aerial putts, profanity and lost golf balls, did participate in the annual Mt. Dundas Open, the world's northernmost golf tournament (76°32' North Latitude). Let it also be known that this task of questionable sanity was accomplished despite near-freezing temperatures, numerous patches of casual Arctic water (snow drifts) and the threat of 18 mph phase winds descending upon the participants with little warning. It is, therefore, with tears in our eyes and fear of certain retribution of Nanok of the North, that we designed do hereby attest that this deed was truly done.

500-Year-Old Scotch

The golf course that is the prototype for all others is the "Old Course" at St. Andrews in Scotland. Lying on ninety-three and a half wind-blown acres, the desolate course was christened by an archbishop in 1552 as a place where the local community could "play at golf, futball, and schuteing."

The St. Andrews Course wasn't designed by a person but mostly by nature. The sand traps came from sheep burrowing into the sand dunes for shelter from the sea's heavy winds. For centuries, the only grass-cutting at St. Andrews was done by sheep and rabbits. Golf course designers around the world have since gone to great lengths to duplicate artificially what occurred naturally there.

The major golf courses in St. Andrews are not private clubs—they're operated by the Links Management Trust for public benefit.

In 1764, the standard round of golf was established at St. Andrews as eighteen holes.

There is an entertaining myth about how that happened, and then there is the true story. First the myth: The guiding council at St. Andrews determined that there were exactly eighteen shots in a quart of whiskey and figured that, golfers drinking at the rate of a shot a hole, eighteen was the right number.

The true story is more prosaic. The Old Course originally had twenty-two holes (actually, eleven holes played one way, then back). However, in the eighteenth century they rearranged the course, and reduced the number to eighteen, in part to make room to build a clubhouse. Because other golf courses used the Old Course as their prototype, eighteen holes became the standard.

Although St. Andrews' Old Course has eighteen holes, there are only eleven greens. Only the first, ninth, seventeenth, and eighteenth have their own greens; the rest share a green with another. The second hole shares with the sixteenth, the third with the fifteenth, and so on, the two numbers always adding up to eighteen.

The Old Course is so "classic" that Sam Snead—accustomed to the overly green, fussily manicured lawns of American golf courses—wondered the first time he saw it in 1946 if it were an abandoned golf course.

Unfortunately, Snead wondered that out loud, offending his hosts. Worse, he brought the wrath of his caddies down on him. They tried to undermine his game by whistling when he was putting, quitting at inopportune times, showing up drunk, and giving him wrong clubs. Nonetheless, Snead managed to win the tournament by four strokes.

The Old Course is the most famous, but it's only one of five golf courses at St. Andrews. There are also the "New" Course (created in 1895), the Jubilee (1897), the Eden (1914), and the Strathtyrum (1993).

fifteen

The Play's the Thing

" Prayer never works for me on the golf course. That may have something to do with my being a terrible putter."

—*The Rev. Billy Graham*

"I'm a golfer, not an athlete."

—*Lee Westwood*

"Golf is the most over-taught and least-learned human endeavor. If they taught sex the way they teach golf, the race would have died out years ago."

—*Jim Murray,* Golf Magazine

There Are Few Atheists in a Bunker: A poll found that, whether religious or not,

75 percent of professional golfers admitted to praying on the golf course.

"**P**ick up the ball and have the clubs destroyed immediately."

> —*Viscount Castleross to his caddy*
> *after a series of bad shots*

A golf course is about the last place you want to be during a thunderstorm. Ask Lee Trevino, who was struck by lightning during the 1975 Western Open: "There was a thunderous crack like cannon fire and suddenly I was lifted a foot and a half off the ground. 'Damn,' I thought to myself, 'this is a helluva penalty for slow play.' " Trevino's advice about surviving a lightning storm?

"Hold up a 1-iron and walk. Even God can't hit a 1-iron." Don't really try it, of course—he was joking.

"The least thing upsets him on the links. He misses short putts because of the uproar of the butterflies in the adjoining meadows."

> —*P. G. Wodehouse, describing*
> *a very sensitive golfer*

"That little white ball won't move 'til you hit it, and there's nothing you can do after it's gone."

> —*Babe Didrikson Zaharias*

"It took me seventeen years to get 3,000 hits in baseball. I did it in one afternoon on the golf course."

—*Hank Aaron, Baseball Hall of Famer*

"The hardest shot is a mashie at 90 yards from the green where the ball has to be played against an oak tree, bounces back into a sand trap, hits a stone, bounces on the green, and then rolls into the cup. The shot is so difficult I have made it only once."

—*Zeppo Marx*

"The hardest shot in golf? I find it to be the hole-in-one."

—*Groucho Marx*

"There are two reasons for making a hole-in-one. The first is that it is immensely laborsaving."

—*H. I. Phillips, writer/composer*

"I was three over—one over a house, one over a patio, and one over a swimming pool."

—*George Brett, baseball star*

"I've heard of unplayable lies, but on the tee?"

—*Bob Hope*

"We're playing a game where the aim is to be below par. It's so wrong for me."

—*Stephanie Vanderkellen,*
character on the TV show Newhart

Golf historians credit the late Tommy Armour, a winner of both the U.S. and British Open championships, with coining the word *yips* to describe the condition of so-called putter's block. He described the yips as "that ghastly time the golfer blacks out, loses sight of the ball and hasn't the remotest idea of what to do with the putter." He wasn't joking—the "yips" forced him into early retirement.

"The average expert player hits 6, 8, or 10 real good shots in a round. The rest are real good misses."

—*Tommy Armour*

Order an extra-large bucket of balls at a driving range and you'll typically get 150 balls. A medium bucket yields 65; a small, 35.

"Playing in the U.S. Open is like tippy-toeing through hell."

—*Jerry McGee*

Double eagles—three strokes under par—are rarer than holes in one. The reason is that holes-in-one are usually made on short holes, requiring only one accurate long shot. A double eagle requires a par-5 hole, meaning that to get one you need to hit two long shots accurately.

The Mile Long Club

I: Harry Leach, on May 26, 1954, hit a drive that went much farther than he'd expected. When he teed off at St. Andrews in Scotland, his ball went out of bounds. When Leach went to find the ball, it seemed the ball had ended up in a dump truck. The dump truck took off and headed straight for the city heap, over a mile away. Let's just say Harry opted to take the penalty instead of play the ball.

II: Nils Lied sounds like a name that begins a tall, tall tale. Instead, sit back and listen to a long one. Nils, a meteorologist from Australia, was camped at base in the Antarctic. Bored with the ice and snow, Nils whiled away the time by practicing his drives and chip shots. On one particular day, the golf gods smiled on Nils and sent his ball a-sliding on the ice. The ball traveled a total of a mile and a half (2,640 yards) before it stopped.

III: Alan Shepard, famous moon golfer, also has the honor of belonging to this very prestigious club. His first shot on the moon went nowhere. His second attempt bounced about 2 feet. His third drive, however, sent his ball flying for miles and miles, says Shepard.

IV: Okay, so this entry's drive didn't technically go a mile, but because it went into the next city, it qualifies as something. Otis Guernsey was at the ninth hole on the Apawanis Golf Club in Rye, New York. When he teed off, his ball shot off in the wrong direction and landed on the eleventh hole . . . of the neighboring Green Meadows Golf Course, in Harrison, New York.

The longest successful putt in the history of the Masters Tournament was made by pro Nick Faldo in 1989. It was a whopping 100 feet long.

sixteen

Playing by the Rules

" **I**t 's good sportsmanship not to pick up golf balls while they are still rolling."

—*Mark Twain*

It used to be that golfers couldn't legally pick up their balls from the green and re-place them with "markers." Maneuvering around other players' balls while putting was considered part of the game. By the 1950s, a couple of pros in tournament de-cided to take advantage of these rules, hit-ting their opponents' balls far afield, as if playing croquet. The rules were soon changed.

"**I**f the following foursome is pressing you, wave them through—and then speed up."

—*Dean Beman*

In 1744, the Magistrates and Council of Edinburgh approved the world's first codified rules and regulations of golf. The "Articles and Laws in Playing Golf—The Rules of the Gentlemen Golfers of Leith" were only thirteen in number. Here they are:

1. You must tee your ball within one club's length of the hole.

2. Your tee must be on the ground.

3. You are not to change the ball which you strike off the tee.

4. You are not to remove stones, bones or any break club for the sake of playing your ball, except on the fair green, and that only within a club's length of your ball.

5. If your ball comes among water, or any watery filth, you are at liberty to take out your ball and bringing it behind the hazard and teeing it, you may play it with any club and

allow your adversary a stroke for so getting out your ball.

6. If your balls be found anywhere touching one another you are to lift the first ball till you play the last.

7. At holeing you are to play your ball honestly for the hole, and not to play upon your adversary's ball, not lying in your way to the hole.

8. If you should lose your ball, by its being taken up, or any other way, you are to go back to the spot where you struck last and drop another ball and allow your adversary a stroke for the misfortune.

9. No man at holeing his ball is to be allowed to mark his way to the hole with his club or anything else.

10. If a ball be stopp'd by any person, horse or dog, or anything else, the ball so stopp'd must be played where it lyes.

11. If you draw your club in order to strike and proceed so far in the stroke as to be bringing down your club; if then your club shall break in any way, it is to be accounted a stroke.

12. He whose ball lyes farthest from the hole is obliged to play first.

13. Neither trench, ditch or dyke made for the preservation of the links, nor the Scholar's Holes or the soldier's lines shall be accounted a hazard but the ball is to be taken out, teed and play'd with any iron club.

It seems like trying to become a virgin again, but it is possible to have your amateur status reinstated by the United States Golf Association (USGA) after going pro. Hundreds of golfers have made the transition back.

However, if you go pro and stay that way for five years, you're ineligible to have your amateur status restored.

No, you can't putt by straddling the ball and hitting it croquet style. That was banned in 1968.

You also can't putt with a pool cue. The USGA forbade the use of pool cues for putting in 1895 after a dispute came up during the U.S. Amateur.

In Professional Golf Association (PGA) tournaments, a player is penalized if he dallies more than 45 seconds before hitting the ball.

Other than glasses or contact lenses, you're not allowed to enhance your vision or better estimate your distance from the hole through the use of a sextant, binoculars, range finder, global positioning system, or any other device.

If you begin your swing and the wind blows your ball off your tee before you can hit it, it still counts as a stroke.

Nowadays, when you hit your ball out of play, you "drop" a ball by holding it out at arm's length and letting go. However, it wasn't always that way. There was a time when you were supposed to drop it over your shoulder. The problem was that the ball would often bounce off the player's body and roll away, so the rule was eventually changed.

According to the official rules of golf, if an opponent asks how many strokes you've taken on a hole, you must tell him or her the truth.

According to the USGA, a player is entitled to relief, or dropping another ball without penalty, if the player's ball comes to rest near a bird's nest and he cannot play the ball without damaging the nest.

A player also gets relief if his or her ball comes to rest in a dangerous situation, for instance, near an alligator, a live rattlesnake, or a bees' nest. Whew!

A player is *not* entitled to relief under USGA rules if his or her ball comes to rest in a *herbally* dangerous situation. If a ball is found within poison ivy, for instance, or poison sumac, a player cannot drop another ball without incurring a penalty. Calamine lotion, anyone?

"**G**o ahead and putt, you are not interrupting my conversation."

—*Robert E. Zorn, golf writer*

Strangely enough, according to PGA rules, you get a two-stroke penalty for

accidentally hitting your partner with a ball
. . . but there's no penalty for hitting anybody else.

You can also get a penalty for acts of God
that occur after addressing your ball but
before your club makes contact with it. Say
you've addressed the ball and the wind or
an earthquake knocks your ball off the tee
before you hit it. That's stroke one.

You're not allowed to wear shorts in PGA
tournaments (or on some golf courses). As
a way to get around the prohibitions,
golfers traditionally wore colorful knickers,
also called "plus fours" because four inches
of fabric were added so that they'd reach
below the knee.

Dress code of the PGA Tour dictates players must wear long pants and collared shirts. In 1992, when Mark Wiebe showed up at the Anheuser Busch Classic in shorts to beat the 102-degree temperature, he was fined $500.

seventeen

Celebrities Open

WILLIAM HOWARD TAFT

*f*red Astaire played golf almost as well as he danced. In his 1938 movie, Carefree, he drove twelve balls while dancing. According to those on the set, they all landed within 8 feet of each other.

Harpo Marx and George Burns once nearly got kicked out of Hillcrest Country Club in Beverly Hills when they played a round of golf in their underwear.

Country singer Willie Nelson has his own golf course, where the rules include:

- No more than twelve to a foursome.
- Change-jingling or wind-letting on the grass is forbidden.

- If you land in rocks, you can take the "Pedernales Stroll" option: picking up your ball and walking it onto the grass.

- USGA rules apply except where you can think of something better.

- Par is how you feel that day. ("I've got one hole that's a par 23," he told an interviewer, "and yesterday I damn near birdied the sucker.")

Kim Jong II, the self-proclaimed "Dear Leader" of North Korea, is apparently quite the golfer. According to the club pro at Pyongyang's golf course in 1994, the dictator shot a 34 during an eighteen-hole game, including the remarkable feat of achieving five holes-in-one.

Comedian Bill Murray, who made a name for himself as a caddy in *Caddyshack,* showed up a few years ago at PGA tournaments to caddy for pro pal Scott Simpson.

You've heard of the Bob Hope and Bing Crosby classics, for sure. You know you're a real golf fanatic, though, if you've heard of all of these past celebrity tourneys:

- The Sammy Davis Greater Hartford Open (1973–1988)
- The Glen Campbell Los Angeles Open (1971–1983)
- The Jamie Farr Toledo Classic (1984)
- The Andy Williams Open (1968–1988)

- The Jackie Gleason Inverrary Classic (1972–1980)
- Dean Martin hosting the Tuscon Open (1973–1975)
- Ed McMahon hosting the Quad City Open (1975–1979)
- Joe Garagiola hosting the Tucson Open (1977–1983)

Actor Barry Fitzgerald, who won the 1944 Academy Award for best supporting actor for his performance in the movie *Going My Way,* had a run in with his Oscar. While practicing his golf swing, he inadvertently knocked the head off of his statue—at the time made of plaster, because the war was on. The Academy graciously gave him a new one. Fitzgerald probably took his practice to the links from that point on.

Hail to the Duffer: Presidents Below Par

The first U.S. president who golfed was William McKinley.

William Taft was president during golf's early days. His avid love of the game is credited with helping popularize it among fellow Americans.

President Taft so loved the game of golf, it's recorded that when his meeting with the president of Chile conflicted with a round of golf he'd arranged earlier, he canceled the meeting and made tee time as scheduled.

President Woodrow Wilson used red golf balls so he could play his beloved game even in the snow.

The very first public golf course to be named after a U.S. president was an eighteen-hole course in San Francisco, which opened in 1925. Harding Park was designed by Scotsman William Watson and named after President Warren G. Harding, another political golf enthusiast.

President Calvin Coolidge didn't make too many long shots on the golf course. As a matter of fact, it's rumored his shots were short because he was afraid of losing one of his golf balls.

President Franklin D. Roosevelt's father had a six-hole golf course built on their family home in Hyde Park, New York, when FDR was just a boy.

Dwight Eisenhower was the president who installed a full putting green on the White House grounds.

If you've ever played the Augusta National in Georgia, you may have run into the Eisenhower Tree, located on the seventeenth hole. It's named for the former president because he asked the course management if they could remove the pine, as he seemed to hit it an awful lot. They refused and made it a monument to him on the course.

Dwight Eisenhower was asked how his golf game had changed after he left the presidency. "A lot more people beat me now."

President John Kennedy may have been the best golfer to ever occupy the White House. However, because he feared the public criticism that Dwight Eisenhower endured for his golfing, he played in near-secrecy during off-hours and away from the public and the press. One day he hit the ball just right and was chagrined to see it heading right for the hole, knowing that the story of the president's hole-in-one would be too good to keep from getting out in the papers. He was relieved when the ball missed the hole by inches.

A set of Kennedy's golf clubs—his Mac-Gregor woods—was auctioned off with Jacqueline Kennedy Onassis's estate in April 1996. They sold for $772,500. His Ben Hogan irons went for a high bid of $387,500 and his putter for $65,750. Besides the clubs, three monogrammed head covers and a stroke counter were sold for a total of $63,250.

"I don't have a handicap. I'm all handicap."
—*President Lyndon B. Johnson*

While in the Oval Office, Nixon often gave autographed golf balls as presidential gifts to friends.

Nixon's vice president Spiro Agnew, who resigned because of corruption, had an equally crooked drive on the golf course. After he beaned several spectators, he had golf balls printed up that said, "You have just been hit by Spiro Agnew."

After President Gerald Ford whacked a few bystanders with untamed drives, Bob Hope quipped, "Gerald Ford made golf a contact sport."

Former president Ronald Reagan loved golf. He was known to practice his chip shots and putts on Air Force One, and even in the Oval Office itself. The story goes that when a reporter once asked Reagan what his handicap was, he replied without hesitation, "Congress." Like much great material, it may have been borrowed—in this case, from former president Lyndon B. Johnson, who had answered the same thing to a reporter years earlier.

Dan Quayle was better at golf than at politics. In fact, some say he would've had better success at becoming a professional golfer, where being perceived as an over-privileged airhead isn't necessarily a handicap. He served as captain of his golf team in college after making a name for himself by shooting a hole-in-one when only seventeen years old. Quayle later defeated professional partner Joey Sindelar by several shots during a pro-am at the Kemper Open. He was on the golf course when he was asked to run for senator, and there again when news of his vice presidential run was announced.

While participating in the 1993 Doug Sanders Celebrity Classic, former president George Bush managed to bean Dan Quayle, his former vice president, on the top of his head. The ball did no apparent damage.

Former president George H. W. Bush has golf in the veins. Not only was his father, Prescott Bush, elected president of the USGA in 1934, but his grandfather, George Herbert Walker, also served as USGA president for a spell. It was this latter Bush who established the amateur Walker Cup.

Professional golfer Tommy Bolt's caddy during a tournament in Hot Springs, Arkansas, was none other than future president Bill Clinton. Clinton loved golf. He could often be seen during his presidency walking the fairways with Secret Service agents, aides, police snipers, special phones, and computers with nuclear codes in tow.

Of all of the golfing presidents, only three are known to have hit holes-in-one: Dwight D. Eisenhower, who hit one shortly before his death, Richard Nixon, and Gerald Ford. Ford, it should be noted, hit not just one but *three* holes-in-one.

eighteen

A Driving Love for the Game

"**G**olf and sex are the only things you can enjoy without being good at them."

—*Jimmy Demaret*

James Hogg, age seventy-seven, collapsed on the first hole of a golf course in Fife, Scotland, and quickly died from a massive heart attack. After a brief pause in the game while an ambulance arrived to take Hogg's body away, the surviving members of his foursome continued their game. "I'm sure Jimmy would've wanted us to do that," intoned his longtime friend and golfing partner.

Similarly, Donald DeGreve, sixty-five, suffered a fatal heart attack on the sixteenth green of a golf course in Winter Haven, Florida. Members of his golfing league respectfully stepped around his sheet-covered body, tastefully skipping from the fifteenth to the seventeenth hole to continue their games. "Life goes on, so we had to keep going," philosophized one.

"It is almost impossible to remember how tragic a place the world is when one is playing golf."

—*Robert Lynd, sociologist*

"Give me golf clubs, fresh air, and a beautiful partner, and you can keep my golf clubs and the fresh air."

—*Jack Benny*

> "If the sun is up, why
> aren't you playing golf?"
>
> —*Lee Trevino*

"I am curiously, disproportionately, unde-servedly happy on a golf course."

—*John Updike*

"The more I see of golf, the more it re-minds me of life. Or, rather, the more I see of life, the more it reminds me of golf."

—*Henry Longhurst*

"When you watch a game, it's fun; when you play a game, it's recreation; but when you work at a game, it's golf."

—*Bob Hope*

"If you want to take long walks, take long walks. If you want to hit things with a stick, hit things with a stick. But there's no excuse for combining the two and putting the results on TV. Golf is not so much a sport as an insult to lawns."

—National Lampoon *(1979)*

"**G**olf is a good walk spoiled."

—*Mark Twain*

"**G**olf has taught me that there is a connection between pain and pleasure. 'Golf' spelled backwards is 'flog.'"

—*Phyllis Diller*

"**I** play with friends, but we don't play friendly games."

—*Ben Hogan*

"**I**sn't it fun to get out on the golf course and lie in the sun?"

—*Bob Hope*

More important than actually spending time with your loved ones: The U.S. Open traditionally plays its final round on Father's Day.

"**G**olf is the most jealous of mistresses."

—*Arnold Haultain*

"**M**y psychiatrist prescribed a game of golf as an antidote to the feelings of euphoria I experience from time to time."

—*Bruce Lansky*

"We learn so many things from golf—how to suffer, for instance."

—Bruce Lansky

"I've had a good day when I don't fall out of the cart."

—Buddy Hackett

"I know I am getting better at golf because I am hitting fewer spectators."

—Gerald Ford

"If you don't succeed at first, don't despair. Remember, it takes time to learn to play golf; most players spend their entire lifetime finding out about the game before they give up."

—*Stephen Baker*

"What other people may find in poetry or art museums, I find in the flight of a good drive."

—*Arnold Palmer*

Acknowledgments

The authors wish to give special thanks to Pamela Sanderson of the USGA Research and Test Center, and to our friends, family members, and all the gang at Conari for their patience and good humor.

Selected References

Associations, Clubs, and Golf-Related Groups
The Environmental News Network
The Global Anti-Golf Movement
The Northern Texas Golf Association
The Scottish Golf Society
The Samford University 1987–1988 golf team
The United States Golf Association

Books

Amazing But True Golf Facts, by Bruce Nash and Allan Zullo. Andrews and McNeel, 1992.

Big Secrets, by William Poundstone. William Morrow & Co. Inc., 1983.

The Compact Edition of the Oxford English Dictionary, 24th Edition. Oxford University Press.

Encyclopaedia Britannica, 15th Edition.

Ever Wonder Why, by Douglas B. Smith. Ballantine Books, 1991.

Golf's Most Wanted, by Floyd Conner. Brassey's, 2001.

How Do Astronauts Scratch and Itch? by David Feldman. Penguin Putnam, Inc., 1997.

Listening to America, by Stuart Berg Flexner. Simon and Schuster, 1982.

Stories Behind Everyday Things, editors of *Reader's Digest.* Reader's Digest Association, Inc., 1980.

Tall Tales of Golf, by the editors of *Golf* magazine. Triumph Books, 1997.

Unauthorized America, by Vince Staten. Harper & Row, Publishers, 1990.

Wannabe Guide to Golf, by Jack Mingo. RDR Books, 1997.

Webster's New World Dictionary, Third College Edition.

What's What, by Reginald Bragonier Jr. and David Fisher. Ballantine Books, 1981.

When Do Fish Sleep? by David Feldman. Harper & Row, Publishers, 1989.

Why Do They Call It a Birdie? by Frank Coffey. Kensington Publishing Corp., 1998.

Magazines, Newspapers, Periodicals

Forbes Magazine
New York Times
Sports Illustrated
Washington City Paper

Web Sites

www.austinsclassicputters.com
www.celebritygolf.com
www.golfballs.com
www.golfeurope.com
www.golfika.com
www.golfonline.com
www.golfsite.com
www.golfsouthidaho.com

indianagolfacademy.com

http://inet.uni2.dk/~i51341/_private/CarlsenRanchV/
tabbreve/dundasgolf.htm

http://lewistowncountryclub.com

www.lpga.com

www.mulligansw.com

www.newsoftheweird.com

www.oldcourse.com

www.pga.com

www.savingsolutions.com

www.spacecom.af.mil

www.straightdope.com

www.tigerwoods.com

www.triadgolf.com

www.usatoday.com

www.usgtf.com/history.htm

www.worldgolf.com

http://world.std.com/~rgu/tigerwoods/tigerwoods.faq

About the Authors

Jen Fariello

Erin Barrett and Jack Mingo have authored twenty books, including *How the Cadillac Got Its Fins, The Couch Potato Guide to Life,* and the bestselling *Just Curious Jeeves* series. They have written articles for many major periodicals, including *Salon,* the *New York Times,* the *Washington Post,* and *Reader's Digest,* and generated more than 30,000 questions for trivia games. Today they live in Charlottesville, Virginia, with kids, a cat, oodles of reference books, two guinea pigs—and nary a golf club in sight.

You can contact Erin and Jack at:
ErinBarrett@earthlink.net
JackMingo@earthlink.net

To Our Readers

If you would like to receive a complete catalog of Conari books, please contact us at:

CONARI PRESS
2550 Ninth Street, Suite 101
Berkeley, California 94710-2551
800-685-9595 • 510-649-7175
fax: 510-649-7190
e-mail: conari@conari.com
www.conari.com